# Keltic Crosses Coloring 2

# Perelandra Design

This "Keltic Crosses Coloring 2" Book contains 18 original drawings of crosses suitable for coloring by any age. Each page also has 8"x10" guidelines for cutting out and framing your finished masterpiece.

## *Books by Kathy O'Meara*

Keltic Crosses Coloring
Keltic Crosses Coloring 2
Keltic Alphabet Coloring: Capital Letters
Keltic Alphabet Coloring: Lower Case Letters
Keltic Coloring: Knots & Numbers
Keltic Coloring: Knotted Nature
Keltic Alphabet Coloring 2: Capital Letters
Keltic Alphabet Coloring 2: Lower Case Letters

### Stained Glass "Window" Patterns

Spring Flowers
Summer Flowers
Autumn
Circle of Life
Keltic Christian

International Standard Book Number

ISBN-13: 978-1724589156
ISBN-10: 1724589156

www.ingramcontent.com/pod-product-compliance
Lightning Source LLC
Chambersburg PA
CBHW080048260726
48658CB00007B/2795